P9-CML-572

I Like the Seasons!

What Happens in Fall?

Sara L. Latta

Enslow Elementary
an imprint of

E **Enslow Publishers, Inc.**

40 Industrial Road   PO Box 38
Box 398   Aldershot
Berkeley Heights, NJ 07922   Hants GU12 6BP
USA   UK

http://www.enslow.com

Chicago Public Library
Gage Park Branch
2807 W. 55th Street
Chicago, IL 60632
(312) 747-0032

Words to Know

harvest (HAR vest)—The food gathered at the end of the growing season.

migrate (MY grate)—To move from one place to another.

season (SEE zuhn)—One of the four parts of the year. Each season has a certain kind of weather.

tilt—To lean to one side.

Earth is tilted.

R0407498101

Contents

Chicago Public Library
Gage Park Branch
2807 W. 55th Street
Chicago, IL 60632
(312) 747 - 0032

What is fall?

There are four seasons of the year. Fall is one of the seasons. The others are winter, spring, and summer.

Each season lasts about three months. Each season has its own kind if weather.

winter   spring   summer

Fall is cooler than summer, but warmer than winter.

fall

Why do we have seasons?

Earth moves around the sun one time each year. Earth **tilts** as it goes around the sun.

Spring in north part of Earth

North Pole tilts toward the sun; it is summer in the north part of Earth.

Summer

The tilt causes more or less sunlight to fall on different parts of Earth.

Winter

Earth's path around sun

North Pole tilts away from sun; it is winter in the north part of Earth.

Winter

As the amount of sunlight changes, the weather changes. So do the seasons.

Summer

Fall in north part of Earth

When does fall start?

Fall starts right after summer. In North America, the first day of fall is around September 21. After this day, the days get cooler. The days also get shorter: The sun sets earlier every day.

Why do leaves change color in fall?

With less sunlight, plants make less food. They get ready to rest for winter. The green part of leaves that makes food goes away.

Now, the leaves show the yellow and orange colors that were hiding behind the green.

What happens to other plants in fall?

In fall, some plants turn brown and look dead. Their roots are still alive, though. Like the trees, they will rest all winter.

purple coneflower in summer and fall

Many plants make seeds or nuts in the fall. Some of these seeds and nuts will grow into new plants in the spring.

Acorns are oak tree seeds.

What do animals do in fall?

In fall, animals get ready for winter. Some grow long, thick fur to keep them warm. Others gather food. Bears eat lots and lots of food in the fall. They will use their fat for energy as they rest over the winter.

Busy squirrels store nuts to eat later.

Why do animals migrate?

Some animals cannot live in the cold winter weather. So in the fall, they migrate to warmer places. Geese and other birds fly south. Many kinds of fish swim to warmer waters.

Monarch butterflies fly thousands of miles to their warm winter homes in Mexico and California.

What do people do in fall?

Many farmers pick their crops in the fall. You may go apple picking or get a Halloween pumpkin. People all around the world celebrate the harvest. In North America, many families share a Thanksgiving feast.

Do leaves need sunlight to change colors?

You will need:

- ❖ tree or shrub that turns colors in the fall (ask an adult to help you find one)
- ❖ heavy paper
- ❖ masking tape

1. In early fall, find a tree with leaves that you know will turn red or purple. A flowering dogwood tree, a maple tree, or a burning bush would work well.

2. Find some leaves that get plenty of sunlight. (Do not pick them.) Tape a piece of paper to part of each leaf.

3. After the leaves have changed color, remove the pieces of paper. Did the part of the leaf under the paper also turn color? Why or why not?

Learn More

Books

Finnegan, Mary Pat. *Autumn: Signs of the Seasons Around North America*. Minneapolis, Minn.: Picture Window Books, 2003.

Florian, Douglas. *Autumnblings*. New York: Greenwillow Press, 2003.

Glaser, Linda, and Susan Swan. *It's Fall*. Minneapolis: Millbrook Press, 2001.

Meyer, Mary L. *Fall*. North Mankato, Minn.: Smart Apple Media, 2003.

Rylant, Cynthia, and Jill Kastner. *In November*. New York: Harcourt Children's Books, 2000.

Web Sites

NASA. *Earth's Seasons*. "What Causes the Seasons?"
<http://kids.msfc.nasa.gov/earth/seasons/
EarthSeasons.asp>
An excellent video describing why the earth has
seasons.

National Oceanic and Atmospheric Administration.
"Migration Concentration."
<http://scijinks.jpl.nasa.gov/noaa/poes_tracking/
index.shtml#>
Play migration concentration to learn more about
migrating animals.

Index

Enslow Elementary, an imprint of Enslow Publishers, Inc.

Enslow Elementary® is a registered trademark of Enslow Publishers, Inc.

Copyright © 2006 by Enslow Publishers, Inc.

All rights reserved.

No part of this book may be reproduced by any means without the written permission of the publisher.

Library of Congress Cataloging-in-Publication Data

Latta, Sara L.
    What happens in fall? / Sara L. Latta.
        p. cm. — (I like the seasons!)
    Includes bibliographical references and index.
    ISBN 0-7660-2417-2 (hardcover)
    1. Autumn—Juvenile literature. 2. Seasons—Juvenile
literature. I. Title. II. Series
    QB637.7.L38 2006
    508.2—dc22
                                    2005012447

Printed in the United States of America

10 9 8 7 6 5 4 3 2 1

To Our Readers: We have done our best to make sure all Internet Addresses in this book were active and appropriate when we went to press. However, the author and the publisher have no control over and assume no liability for the material available on those Internet sites or on other Web sites they may link to. Any comments or suggestions can be sent by e-mail to comments@enslow.com or to the address on the back cover.

Photo Credits: © Adam Jones/Visuals Unlimited, p. 12 (left), Alan & Sandy Carey/Photo Researchers, Inc., p. 14; © Corel Corporation, pp. 4 (spring), 10, 20 (left), 21, 22, 23; Enslow Publishers, Inc., p. 12 (right); © 2005 Frans Lanting, www.lanting.com, p. 17; George Halig / Photo Researchers, Inc., p. 18; George Robinson/IPN/Aurora Photos, p. 9; Jose Azel/Aurora Photos, p. 11; © 2005 JupiterImages Corporation, pp. 4 (summer), 5, 8, 19; © Leroy Simon/Visuals Unlimited, p. 13; © Lightwave Photography, Inc. / Animals Animals, p. 15; Mark Garlick/Science Photo Library, pp. 6–7; © Richard Kolar / Animals Animals, p. 16; © skjoldphotographs.com, p. 4 (winter).

Cover Photo: Richard Hutchings/Photo Researchers, Inc.

Science Consultant
Harold Brooks, Ph.D.
NOAA/National Severe Storms Laboratory
Norman, Oklahoma

Series Literacy Consultant
Allan A. De Fina, Ph.D.
Past President of the New Jersey Reading Association
Professor, Department of Literacy Education
New Jersey City University

Note to Parents and Teachers: The I Like the Seasons! series supports the National Science Education Standards for K–4 science. The Words to Know section introduces subject-specific vocabulary words, including pronunciation and definitions. Early readers may need help with these new words.